People
Around
the
World

T0017292

Life and Culture in
RUSSIA
AND THE EURASIAN REPUBLICS

RYAN WOLF

PowerKiDS
press

Published in 2021 by The Rosen Publishing Group, Inc.
29 East 21st Street, New York, NY 10010

First Edition

Editor: Siyavush Saidian
Book Design: Seth Hughes

Photo Credits: Cover Baturina Yuliya/Shutterstock.com; p. 5 Kostiantyn Fastov/Shutterstock.com; p. 6 Komarenko Svetlana/Shutterstock.com; p. 7 Peter Hermes Furian/Shutterstock.com; p. 8 Lena Safronova/Shutterstock.com p. 9 Timolina/Shutterstock.com; p. 10 EZBE/Shutterstock.com; p. 11 Maxim Petrichuk/Shutterstock.com; p. 13 (top) Boligolov Andrew/Shutterstock.com p. 13 (bottom) SVF2/Contributor/Universal Images Group/Getty Images; p. 14 KIRILL KUDRYAVTSEV/Staff/AFP/Getty Images; p. 15 Kirill Sergeev/Shutterstock.com; p. 16 © istockphoto.com/alejomiranda; p. 17 Melanie Stetson Freeman/Contributor/Christian Science Monitor/Getty Images; p. 20 Adam Jan Figel/Shutterstock.com; p. 21 Heritage Images/Contributor/Hulton Fine Art Collection/Getty Images; p. 22 Wikimedia Commons/Kaganer; p. 23 Matyas Rehak/Shutterstock.com; p. 24 Reidl/Shutterstock.com; p. 26 (top) Wikimedia Commons/ПростоУчастник; p. 26 (bottom) Boris Medvedev/Shutterstock.com p. 27 Wikimedia Commons/Dmitry Rozhkov; p. 29 Courtesy Library of Congress; pp. 30–31 Laski Diffusion/Contributor/Hulton Archive/Getty Images; p. 33 Claude Harris/Stringer/Hulton Archive/Getty Images; p. 34 Sean Gallup/Staff/Getty Images News/Getty Images; p. 35 Time Life Pictures/Contributor/The LIFE Picture Collection/Getty Images; p. 37 TASS/Contributor/TASS/Getty Images; p. 38 Movie Poster Image Art/Contributor/Moviepix/Getty Images; p. 41 Focus On Sport/Contributor/Focus on Sport/Getty Images; p. 42 (left) Clive Brunskill/Staff/Hulton Archive/Getty Images; p. 42 (right) Alexander Shcherbak/Contributor/TASS/Getty Images; p. 43 Viktor Drachev/Contributor/TASS/Getty Images; p. 44 Bernie Nunez/Contributor/Getty Images Sport/Getty Images.

Cataloging-in-Publication Data

Names: Wolf, Ryan.
Title: Life and culture in Russia and the Eurasian Republics / Ryan Wolf.
Description: New York : PowerKids Press, 2021. | Series: People around the world | Includes glossary and index.
Identifiers: ISBN 9781725321649 (pbk.) | ISBN 9781725321663 (library bound) | ISBN 9781725321656 (6 pack) | ISBN 9781725321670 (ebook)
Subjects: LCSH: Russia (Federation)-Juvenile literature. | Russia (Federation)-Social life and customs-Juvenile literature. | Russia (Federation)-Social conditions-Juvenile literature.
Classification: LCC DK510.23 W64 2021 | DDC 947-dc23

Manufactured in the United States of America

CPSIA Compliance Information: Batch #CSPK20: For Further Information contact Rosen Publishing, New York, New York at 1-800-237-9932

Find us on

Contents

Introduction **4**
The USSR and Beyond

Chapter 1 .... **6**
Clothing, Food, and Shelter

Chapter 2 .... **12**
Language and Religion

Chapter 3 .... **18**
Art and Architecture

Chapter 4 .... **25**
Folklore and Literature

Chapter 5 .... **32**
Music, Dance, and Film

Chapter 6 .... **39**
Sports and Games

Glossary **46**

For More Information **47**

Index **48**

Introduction
THE USSR AND BEYOND

T hroughout history, the people of Russia and the Eurasian **republics** have made valuable cultural contributions to humanity. From the 16th to the 19th century, Russia grew from a small kingdom in eastern Europe to the largest country (in terms of landmass) on Earth. Its borders combined sections of Europe and Asia, mixing cultural elements from both continents. Russia also conquered many of its neighbors, which have become today's independent Eurasian republics.

From 1922 to 1991, Russia and the other Eurasian republics were part of the Union of Soviet Socialist Republics (USSR), or Soviet Union, under a **Communist** government. The government operated a **command economy** run by state planners. Under the **dictatorship**

command economy: Economy in which the government controls all production and distribution of goods and services.

republic: A form of government in which people elect representatives

of Joseph Stalin, populations were forcefully moved and millions were imprisoned,

The matryoshka, or Russian nesting doll, is one of the most famous symbols of Russian culture.

executed, or starved to death. Through rapid industrialization, the Soviet Union became one of the world's mightiest powers. It competed with the United States during the Cold War period from about 1947 to 1991.

In 1991, the Soviet Union ended and Russia experienced a **transition** to a more **limited government**. Many of the Eurasian republics became independent states. In eastern Europe, these states are Belarus, Estonia, Latvia, Lithuania, Moldova, and Ukraine. In central Asia, countries include Kazakhstan, Kyrgyzstan, Tajikistan, Turkmenistan, and Uzbekistan. The Caucasus mountain region features the states of Armenia, Azerbaijan, and Georgia. Each of these countries has its own unique lifestyles and forms of cultural expression.

1 CLOTHING, FOOD, AND SHELTER

Society in Russia and the Eurasian republics is **multicultural**, as these countries are home to people of many different **ethnicities**. These ethnic groups express themselves through a variety of clothing, types of food, and styles of shelter. Major ethnic groups in the region are the Slavic people of eastern Europe and Russia and the Turkic peoples of central Asia. Other ethnicities include the Tatars, who are of Turkic and Mongol descent, and the Tajiks, who are of Persian descent.

This girl is dressed in Slavic clothing featuring popular patterns that have been used for centuries.

This map highlights the location—and large size—of Russia and its neighboring Eurasian republics.

Slavic culture includes pieces of traditional clothing like the *rubakha*, an oversized shirt that often features a colorful lining. Eastern European headscarves are often called babushkas. In Russia, the literal meaning of the word "babushka" is "grandmother." Today, due

A woman in Uzbekistan is dressed in the traditional clothing of wealthy Tatars. Some people in Kazakhstan, Ukraine, Uzbekistan, and Russia are of Tatar ancestry.

to **cultural diffusion**, most people in Russia and eastern Europe wear Western clothing. Wool and fur coats are common across the region because of the cold weather.

Some Russian and eastern European recipes are echoes of the **traditional economies** in the region, which often relied on **subsistence farming**. Russian dishes include borscht, beef stroganoff, and appetizers called zakuska. Other regional favorites are stuffed dumplings known as *vareniki* in Russia and pierogi in eastern Europe. Russia is also famous for vodka, an alcohol generally made from potatoes.

CULTURAL CONNECTIONS

In central Asia, there's a popular traditional drink made from **fermented** horse or camel milk. The beverage, called koumiss, dates back to ancient regional tribes.

Borscht

Borscht is a beet soup eaten widely throughout Russia and eastern Europe. This Slavic dish can be served hot or cold. It's often topped with sour cream and dill garnish. In Russia and Ukraine, borscht typically includes beef, cabbage, and other vegetables. Some recipes feature potatoes and mushrooms or don't contain meat. Borscht is well known for its bright red color and sweet beet flavoring. In order to balance out the sweetness, sometimes vinegar or kvass is added to the dish. Kvass is a weak alcoholic drink made from fermented bread.

Borscht, a popular beet soup, is eaten throughout eastern Europe and Russia. It's made using different recipes.

Traditional Russian-style country homes are called isbas. These log houses can be constructed without nails. Portable dwellings among **nomadic** native tribes in Russia and the Eurasian republics include *chums, yarangas,* and yurts. Igloos, made from ice blocks, are still used in Russia's far northeastern region among the native Inuit people.

A woman dressed in a rubakha serves a plate of vareniki (pierogies) with sour cream and onions.

In central Asia, a coat called a *chapan* is traditionally worn in the winter. The *tubeteika*, a type of cap, is also widespread. Historically, central Asian food uses a lot of meat, including sheep, goat, and horse. Rice pilaf dishes have also become widespread, as well as Turkic dumplings known as *manti*.

CULTURAL CONNECTIONS

A samovar is a metal container used to boil water. Many households in Russia and the Eurasian republics rely on samovars to make tea and other hot drinks.

Until recently, yurts were a common form of housing in central Asia for those who lived outside of cities. During the 20th century, the

Yurts

For thousands of years, nomadic people on the Eurasian steppe have lived in round tents called yurts. Horses or small wagons traditionally transported these tents. Steppe warrior tribes camped in yurts as their armies passed through Europe and Asia. While there are few remaining nomadic tribes today, the yurt is still an important part of central Asian culture. Yurts are made of flexible wooden poles and are commonly covered in wool felt. The top of the yurt is left partly open to allow space for a chimney. Inside, a yurt is often decorated with colorful carpets and ornaments.

Yurts like the domed tent pictured here have existed for thousands of years. The yurt is the national dwelling of Kazakhstan and Kyrgyzstan.

nomadic way of life was nearly wiped out by the Soviet Union. In this era, many apartment buildings and farm homes were constructed.

2 LANGUAGE AND RELIGION

People of the many different cultures of the world are often defined—at least partially—by their religious beliefs and the languages they speak. Religions serve as models for how humans should live and behave. They also offer ways for people to make sense of the world and find greater meaning. However, faith can lead to conflict, since religious ideas sometimes oppose one another. Language gives people a way to communicate, helping groups cooperate and overcome disagreement. Like religion, languages help people think about the world. Religion and language have inspired both cooperation and **controversy** in the history of Russia and the Eurasian republics.

controversy: Argument or division.

Since AD 988, many Russians have been followers of Eastern Orthodox Christianity. The patriarch of Moscow leads the Russian Orthodox Church. A breakaway group of Russian Orthodox Christians, called Old Believers, resisted reforms made by the church in the 17th century. During the Soviet era, the Communist leadership believed religious ideas didn't fit in with their politics. The government shut down many Christian and non-Christian religious sites and killed some religious leaders. After the Soviet Union collapsed, religious freedom greatly increased.

This detailed ceiling at the Church of the Savior on Spilled Blood in Saint Petersburg, Russia, depicts stories of the Christian faith. The church was built over the spot where Tsar Alexander II was assassinated, or killed, in 1881.

Some native tribes in the Russian region of northern Siberia continue to take part in traditional pre-Christian religious practices like **shamanism**

shamanism: A religion based on interaction with a spirit world.

Eastern Orthodoxy

Eastern Orthodoxy is a form of Christianity. Christians follow the teachings of Jesus of Nazareth, a Jewish preacher executed, or killed, during the first century AD. Orthodox Christians believe that God took on human form through Jesus, overcoming death and providing a path to new life. Through the process of *theosis*, Orthodox believers seek to become more like God. Eastern Orthodox traditions are based on the Christian Bible, church fathers, and agreements made by official councils. The Eastern Orthodox Church was united with the Roman Catholic Church until 1054, when the groups split over religious differences. Countries where Orthodoxy is prominent have their own regional leaders called patriarchs.

Kirill, the patriarch of Moscow in 2019, leads a Russian Orthodox religious ceremony. The patriarch is selected by a council called the Holy Synod.

Most people in central Asia practice Islam. Historically, Russia generally allowed Muslim believers to practice their faith in regions it conquered. There have, however, been periods of

Islam

Islam is a **monotheistic** religion that arose on the Arabian Peninsula during the seventh century. Muslims, or followers of Islam, obey teachings they believe God revealed to the prophet Muhammad. Their holy book is called the Qur'an. The Five Pillars of Islam teach that all Muslims should profess their faith, perform prayers five times daily, give to charity, fast during the month of Ramadan, and travel to the holy city of Mecca at least once, if possible. Islam quickly spread throughout central Asia. Important religious sites, such as Bukhara and Samarkand in Uzbekistan, helped expand early Islamic thought.

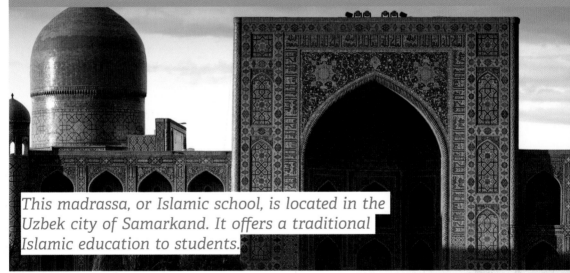

This madrassa, or Islamic school, is located in the Uzbek city of Samarkand. It offers a traditional Islamic education to students.

religious tension and violence in the region. The Chechnya region of Russia, which is mostly Muslim, has had a troubled relationship with Russia's central government since the end of the Soviet Union.

monotheistic: Having to do with belief in one god.

CYRILLIC
ALPHABET

А Б В Г Д Е
Ё Ж З И Й К
Л М Н О П Р
С Т У Ф Х Ц
Ч Ш Щ Ъ Ы Ь
Э Ю Я

The Cyrillic alphabet is used for more than 50 languages spoken throughout Russia, eastern Europe, and central Asia. It has 33 letters representing slightly different sounds than those found in English.

The main language groups in Russia and the Eurasian republics are Slavic and Turkic. Russia, Ukraine, and Belarus all share similar Slavic languages. Turkic languages are spoken throughout central Asia in countries such as Azerbaijan, Kazakhstan, Kyrgyzstan, Turkmenistan, and Uzbekistan. Other Eurasian countries have their own language histories.

CULTURAL CONNECTIONS

Full Russian names include a middle name that's a patronymic. A patronymic references the name of the person's father. This is done for both males and females.

In the 19th and early 20th centuries, the Russian government tried to impose the Russian language on many places it ruled. This process was called Russification.

The Russian language is taught in all public schools in Russia. The Russian public education system is broken into primary, basic, and secondary education, with most students attending school for 11 to 12 years.

However, because language can be such an important part of an ethnic group's cultural identity, this policy was deeply unpopular. Ukraine and Belarus split from Russia in 1991 in part because of language differences. In 2014, some Russian-speaking rebel groups in Ukraine sided with Russia when it captured Ukraine's Crimean Peninsula.

CULTURAL CONNECTIONS

The Turkish alphabet has the unique letters Ç, Ğ, İ, Ö, Ş, and Ü. The letter C is pronounced like "jay," while Ç makes a "ch" sound.

3 ART AND ARCHITECTURE

Art has long been a major part of Eurasian culture. Some people from the region still practice ancient forms of folk art. Central Asia, especially, is noted for its colorful carpet and blanket designs. Slavic art styles in Russia and eastern Europe include detailed approaches to painting, such as in *khokhloma* (paintings on wood) and *pysanky* (paintings on Easter eggs). Special cloths called *rushnyks* are featured in weddings and funerals. First created in 1890, the *matryoshka* doll (nesting doll) quickly became one of the most celebrated imports from Russian culture.

CULTURAL CONNECTIONS

Islamic art in central Asia features geometric patterns and shapes. Many Muslims believe that painting or sculpting a human image would make them guilty of the sin of **idolatry**.

Slavic Folk Art

MATRYOSHKA
Russian Nesting Dolls

KHOKHLOMA
Wood Painting Pattern

PYSANKY
Ukrainian Easter Eggs

Art forms that are distinctly Russian and eastern European in style have found audiences all over the world.

Medieval art in Russia focused largely on religious subjects and historical recording. Realism, or making art look like real life, wasn't important to Russian art, since the focus was on conveying meaning, not on capturing the exact details of life. During the 17th and 18th centuries, due to European influence, portrait painters and other realistic artists became popular among the noble class. Russian Ilya Repin (1844–1930) is recognized as one of the most accomplished realist artists of the 19th century.

Icons

Orthodox Christians use religious images called icons to focus their attention on spiritual ideas. These images are typically small and square, featuring pictures of holy figures or Christian stories on painted wood. The art of the Byzantine Empire greatly influenced the style of Russian icons. Careful use of symbolism and color is important to send certain religious messages. Some Orthodox Christians believe icons have inspired miracles by helping believers focus on their prayers. For centuries, Orthodox Christians have kept smaller icons in their homes, and larger icons are displayed in Orthodox churches.

This icon of the Holy Trinity was designed by medieval painter Andrei Rublev during the early 15th century.

During the early 20th century, the Russian avant-garde, or experimental, movement led to new (abstract) art forms. Russian futurism was based on industrial and **urban** imagery, seeking to convey a sense of motion and speed. Constructivism

Space Force Construction (1921) by Lyubov Popova is an example of the Russian avant-garde style.

involved bringing clear, often angular shapes together in new and colorful ways. Many avant-garde artists hoped to support the Soviet Union through (propaganda). However, when Joseph Stalin came to power, he shut down their work, preferring more realistic art styles.

CULTURAL CONNECTIONS

Lavras are series of caves or cells where Orthodox monks live. The Trinity Lavra of Saint Sergius in Russia and the Kiev Pechersk Lavra in Ukraine are major religious sites featuring beautiful architecture.

abstract: Describing art that expresses ideas non-realistically.
propaganda: Art, written materials, or ideas that are spread to support a government or cause and are often false or misleading.

Soviet Propaganda

To spread messages supporting their government's political vision, the Soviets developed their own propaganda. Since access to outside information was heavily limited and **censored** in the USSR, many Soviet citizens relied on this propaganda to learn about the world. Visual propaganda generally featured red and yellow colors, mirroring the Soviet flag. Images often encouraged citizens to be good workers. They also featured figures such as Russian leaders Vladimir Lenin and Joseph Stalin as heroes of the people. This encouraged national pride even during times of economic difficulty and political oppression.

Works of public propaganda art were meant to inspire citizens to take pride in the Soviet government.

ДЕЛУ ОТЦО
ВЕРНЫ !

The Heart of Chechnya is a mosque in Grozny, built in 2008. It's a center of Islam in southwestern Russia. Its towers, known as minarets, are used during calls to prayer.

Many great works of architecture have been built in Russia and the Eurasian republics. Older medieval buildings include Orthodox cathedrals, churches, and monasteries. During the reign of Peter the Great (1672–1725), Western architectural influence took over traditional Eastern forms. Government buildings, such as the Winter Palace, were designed to look similar to those found in European courts. Under Catherine the Great (1729–1796), the State Hermitage Museum was built in Saint Petersburg. It contains the world's second-largest public art collection.

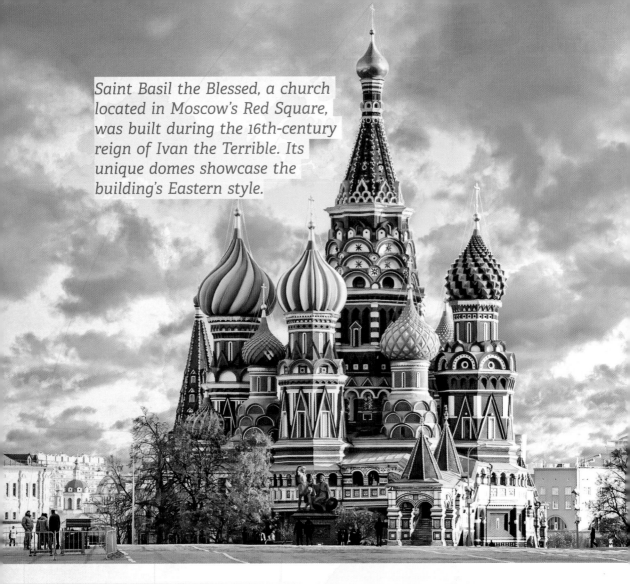

Saint Basil the Blessed, a church located in Moscow's Red Square, was built during the 16th-century reign of Ivan the Terrible. Its unique domes showcase the building's Eastern style.

During the time of the Soviet Union, architecture focused on function and utility, with some experiments in geometric design. Major works of Soviet architecture include the Narkomfin collective living complex in Moscow and the National Library in Minsk, Belarus.

4
FOLKLORE AND LITERATURE

T he lands of Russia and the Eurasian republics contain rich and varied literary traditions. In the Caucasus mountain range, the Nart sagas—similar to Greek myths—were passed down for centuries. Throughout central Asia, Muslim poets and philosophers, such as Ali Shir Nava'i (1441–1501), developed unique styles and thoughts. Russia developed a tradition of heroic poetry, religious writing, and folktales but didn't become internationally known for its literature until the late 18th century.

The first half of the 19th century is considered Russia's golden age of poetry. Writers such as Mikhail Lermontov and Aleksandr Pushkin mixed **folklore**, fairy tales,

folklore: Traditional customs, beliefs, stories, and sayings.

In Russian fairy tales, Baba Yaga is a witch who lives in a house perched on giant hen's legs. She is known to eat people, but can also provide magical gifts.

One of Russia's most influential poets, Aleksandr Pushkin (1799–1837) is seen as a father of modern Russian literature.

heroic drama, and nature into their poems. Major works of fiction from this era include Pushkin's *Eugene Onegin* (1833), a novel written in poetic verse, and *Dead Souls* (1842), comedic **satire** by Nikolai Gogol.

The mid–19th century saw this region's styles turn toward realistic writing that addressed social issues. World-renowned authors Fyodor Dostoyevsky, Leo Tolstoy, and Ivan Turgenev tackled philosophical, religious,

Fyodor Dostoyevsky

One of Russia's greatest authors, Fyodor Dostoyevsky was active in revolutionary politics as a young man. After he was almost executed for his behavior, he spent years in a Siberian prison camp. When he returned home, Dostoyevsky wrote complex novels about characters struggling with religion, morality, and the search for meaning and purpose. Dostoyevsky often wrote about his concern that people in Russia were replacing their Christian beliefs with a new faith in violent political ideas. His famous novels include *Notes from the Underground* (1864), *Crime and Punishment* (1866), *The Idiot* (1869), *The Possessed* (1872), and *The Brothers Karamazov* (1880).

Fyodor Dostoyevsky (1821–1881) helped develop the modern psychological novel. His works often focused on the inner mental states of characters, exploring how ideas influenced their actions.

and political issues in their detailed novels. In the early 20th century, some writers, including Andrey Bely and Mikhail Bulgakov, took literature in more **surreal** and symbolic directions. Others, like Anton Chekhov and Maxim Gorky, continued the realist approach. Chekhov is recognized today as one of the best short story writers of all time.

Eras of Russian Literature

FOLKTALES AND RELIGIOUS LITERATURE
(pre-18th century)

GOLDEN AGE OF RUSSIAN LITERATURE
(19th century)

SOVIET ERA LITERATURE
(1922–1991)

POST-SOVIET LITERATURE
(since 1991)

Russian literary styles and priorities have evolved during each new era. These changes reflected shifting societal values and concerns.

Some authors wrote fiction to encourage revolutionary action. Nikolay Chernyshevsky's novel *What Is to Be Done?* (1863) inspired many people to enter radical politics. When

Leo Tolstoy

Leo Tolstoy grew up in a noble family and wrote lengthy novels about Russian history and culture, including *War and Peace* (1869) and *Anna Karenina* (1878). He became famous and was seen globally as the foremost figure in Russian literature. As Tolstoy grew older, he began to identify more with his Christian faith and with the Russian peasantry despite his noble background. His later works, such as *The Kingdom of God Is Within You* (1894), explore his philosophy of Christian **socialism**.

Leo Tolstoy (1847–1910), the author of War and Peace, *is pictured in simple peasant's clothing toward the end of his life. Although from a wealthy family, Tolstoy chose to live in a peasant community because of his religious beliefs.*

Communist revolutionaries eventually took power in Russia, they quickly censored any art they considered anti-revolutionary. They argued that censorship was necessary to keep society on the Communist path.

In the Soviet era, many authors—including the influential Aleksandr Solzhenitsyn—were arrested and forced to work in labor camps like this.

In the Soviet Union, some writers were exiled, thrown in prison, or killed. When the Soviet Union became slightly more open in the 1960s, people in Russia and the Eurasian republics began to write about the ugly sides of life under the Soviet government. For example, Aleksandr Solzhenitsyn

CULTURAL CONNECTIONS

Mikhail Bulgakov's fantasy novel *The Master and Margarita* (completed 1940; published 1967) famously detailed how the author believed writing his book still mattered even if Soviet censors never let it be published.

spent nearly a decade in a gulag labor camp for insulting Stalin in a letter to a friend. He described his prison experience in the novel *One Day in the Life of Ivan Denisovich* (1962) and in his nonfiction *Gulag Archipelago* (1973). Western governments used these works and others to criticize the Soviets.

CULTURAL CONNECTIONS

American author Vladimir Nabokov (1899–1977) spent his early life in pre-revolutionary Russia. As a United States citizen, he wrote groundbreaking and controversial works such as *Lolita* (1955) and *Pale Fire* (1962).

5
MUSIC, DANCE, AND FILM

F orms of traditional music and dance remain significant parts of Russian and Eurasian culture. Folk music and songs of religious worship have long provided people with meaning and joy.

Traditional Eurasian Musical Instruments

BALALAIKA
Russia

DOMBRA
Kazakhstan

DUDUK
Armenia

MUGHAM TRIO
Azerbaijan

Eurasian folk music traditions use their own native instruments to produce unique styles and sounds.

Unique instruments can be found among different ethnic groups around Eurasia, each of which offers its own approaches to the performing arts.

French ballet spread to Russia during the 18th century. The art form was perfected at places such as Moscow's Bolshoi Theatre. Russia has produced many great ballet dancers, including Vaslav Nijinski, Rudolf Nureyev, and Anna Pavlova.

Anna Pavlova (1881–1931) was Russia's most influential ballerina. She performed her popular solo piece "Dance of the Dying Swan" more than 4,000 times. Pavlova also created a company that toured the globe.

Ukrainian folk dancers are shown here performing, bringing to life one of the many traditional types of dance found in the Eurasian republics.

During the 19th century, a group of **composers** known as the Five dedicated themselves to making classical music that sounded distinctly Russian. Their works included ballets and operas, such as Nikolay Rimsky-Korsakov's *Scheherazade* (1888). Influential 19th-century composers included Mikhail Glinka, Modest Mussorgsky, and Pyotr Ilyich Tchaikovsky. In the 20th century, Sergey Prokofiev, Sergey Rachmaninoff, Dmitry Shostakovich, and Igor Stravinsky all greatly impacted the development of classical music, both regionally and globally.

CULTURAL CONNECTIONS

The 1913 premiere of *The Rite of Spring* by Russian composer Igor Stravinsky (1882–1971) nearly led to a riot because the audience hated its experimental style. The ballet is now considered an all-time great.

Tchaikovsky Worldwide

Pyotr Ilyich Tchaikovsky is one of the world's most well-known composers. His ballet *The Nutcracker* (1892) is often performed during the Christmas season.

Tchaikovsky's other ballets, *Swan Lake* (1876) and *The Sleeping Beauty* (1890), remain incredibly popular and are also widely performed. Other famous compositions include *Piano Concerto No. 1* (1875) and *The 1812 Overture* (1880). Though Tchaikovsky is Russia's most recognized composer today, he was often criticized during his lifetime. Many Russians felt that his music sounded too European and didn't properly honor the Russian tradition. Others noticed that the quality of Tchaikovsky's music would appeal to everyone.

Pyotr Ilyich Tchaikovsky (1840–1893) is one of the most popular figures in the history of classical music. His ballets and other musical pieces are performed around the world every year.

In the Soviet Union, people often produced music to serve the needs of the government. Popular Western music was mostly banned. During the post-Soviet era, the Russian pop band t.A.T.u found international success. Other Eurasian countries also produced talent in pop and rock. For example, members of the alternative metal band System of a Down are of Armenian descent.

CULTURAL CONNECTIONS

Peter and the Wolf by Sergei Prokofiev (1891–1953) was adapted into a Disney animated short in 1946. Walt Disney's *Fantasia* (1940) also featured compositions by Stravinsky, Mussorgsky, and Tchaikovsky.

Russian filmmakers, even during the Soviet era, deeply affected the global history of cinema. Directors such as Sergey Eisenstein, Vsevolod Pudovkin, and Dziga Vertov made technical and artistic improvements to cinema that were imitated worldwide. After Joseph Stalin's death in 1953, Soviet films received even more attention abroad.

Sergey Eisenstein

Sergey Eisenstein fought in the Communist Red Army during the Russian Civil War. After gaining the trust of the Soviet government, he received permission to make historical films. Eisenstein developed original ideas about how motion pictures should be shot and produced. One of his most important concepts was the **montage**, which involves piecing together different images to convey an overall idea. This technique, which can be seen in Hollywood movies today, helped the flow of motion pictures. Eisenstein's most famous film, *Battleship Potemkin* (1925), used montages to make key scenes more interesting. Eisenstein's later pictures featured musical scores by Sergey Prokofiev and occasionally faced censorship.

Soviet director Sergey Eisenstein (1898–1948) provided a new language for filmmakers.

Award-winning pictures included war films like *The Cranes Are Flying* (1957) and *Come and See* (1985). In the 1960s and 1970s, director Andrey Arsenyevich Tarkovsky made art films featuring religious subjects. He eventually left the Soviet Union to escape censorship.

This poster is for the science fiction art film Solaris (1972), directed by Andrei Arsenyevich Tarkovsky. The Soviet government sometimes censored his films.

Since the fall of the Soviet Union, Russian films have met some success overseas. The vampire thriller *Night Watch* (2004) was an international hit, leading to a Hollywood career for director Timur Bekmambetov. Russian television has also grown in appeal, releasing original dramas and comedies. RT, a Russian news network, broadcasts in the United States.

6

SPORTS AND GAMES

Sports and games have brought people in Russia and the Eurasian republics together throughout history. Due to increasing **globalization** over the past century, many sports played in the region are the same as those in the West. Soccer is the most popular sport in several Eurasian countries, including Russia. In most parts of the world, soccer is known as football.

CULTURAL CONNECTIONS

Many ski resorts are located along the Trans-Siberian Railway, a train line that travels across Russia. It takes about six days to ride from Moscow to Russia's Pacific coast.

Traditional Eurasian Sports

GORODKI
Similar to bowling and horseshoes
RUSSIA

GUSHTIGIRI
National form of wrestling
TAJIKISTAN

KOKPAR
Goat hockey (also known as buzkashi)
KAZAKHSTAN

SALBURUN
Hunting sport involving archery and falconry
KYRGYZSTAN

Eurasian countries are home to many unique sports, with some dating back thousands of years.

Because of their colder climate, Russia and eastern Europe have earned reputations for producing athletes who excel in winter games. Their countries are well represented in ice hockey, figure skating, and the biathlon, a sport that combines cross-country skiing with rifle shooting. Bandy, a winter sport similar to hockey, is also popular in the region. Many

Olympics and the Cold War

During the Cold War, Soviet athletes competed with Western countries in events such as the Olympics. The Soviet Union had a reputation for athletic excellence, winning 80 gold medals in total. Sometimes, Soviet and eastern European athletes fled their countries during sports competitions, **defecting** to other nations. One of the most famous Olympic showdowns between the Soviet Union and the United States was the Miracle on Ice hockey game in 1980. The game took place during the Winter Olympics in Lake Placid, New York. In it, a youthful American hockey team shockingly defeated the four-time gold-medal–winning Soviet team.

The U.S. hockey team defeated the more accomplished Soviet team during the 1980 Olympic Winter Games.

teams in North America's National Hockey League (NHL) often hire Russian and Eurasian athletes to play for them.

CULTURAL CONNECTIONS

Russia has had multiple doping, or drug, scandals related to the Olympics. Some athletes have been caught using performance-enhancing drugs that give them an unfair advantage over their competition.

Russian tennis player Anna Kournikova became a celebrity for winning Grand Slam doubles tournaments with tennis partner Martina Hingis. She now lives in the United States.

Lapta is one of Russia's oldest sports. The game, which arose in the 10th century, combines aspects of cricket and baseball.

In central Asia, many native sports arose from the ancient nomadic cultures that populated the area. Since 2014, the World Nomad Games have been held every two years. Competitions include horse racing, wrestling, archery, falconry, and *kokpar*, a form of hockey on horseback involving the body of a goat.

A woman fires a bow and arrow with her legs at the World Nomad Games. In the background, yurts are set up for the competitors.

The board games chess, checkers, and backgammon have been popular in Russia, eastern Europe, and central Asia for centuries. In ancient times, people made sets of dice from animal bones. Board games native to Central Asia include *toguz korgool*, a board game involving stones. In Russia, *durak* and *preferans* are popular card games.

Kasparov vs. Deep Blue

Russian Garry Kasparov was once the world chess champion. In 1997, Kasparov played a chess match against IBM supercomputer Deep Blue. During a six-game match, Kasparov won once, Deep Blue won twice, and three games ended in ties. Deep Blue's victory revealed how technology could be programmed to outperform human experts. Some saw this as a frightening moment that suggested all aspects of human life could one day be replaced by computers.

Nf6 10. Bg2

Many believed Garry Kasparov to be the world's greatest chess player. He was defeated by the IBM computer Deep Blue in a 1997 chess tournament.

Since the late 20th century, video games have spread across the globe. Soviet **software** engineer Alexey Leonidovich Pajitnov invented *Tetris*–one of the world's most played games– in 1985. Many Russians and Eurasians today connect to the world through video games, playing alongside people from all over the world.

As tensions rise between Russia, its Eurasian neighbors, and the world, games and sports remain important outlets through which people can meet for friendly competition. Games often help people–especially from a region as unique and varied as Eurasia–look beyond differences in language, religion, and politics. They enable groups to see one another's skills and talents, recognizing a humanity that goes beyond cultural divisions.

CULTURAL CONNECTIONS

The COVID-19 global pandemic, which started in 2019, challenged the health, daily lives, celebrations, and sports culture of people in this region and the wider world.

GLOSSARY

censor: To remove certain subjects or images from media because they are considered offensive or harmful.

Communist: Describing the political party and economic system of the USSR and Russia.

cultural diffusion: The process of spreading cultural traits from one region to another.

dictatorship: A system of government in which a single ruler has all the power.

fermented: Having gone through a chemical change that results in the production of alcohol.

globalization: The development of an increasingly connected global economy marked by free trade and free flow of capital.

idolatry: Worshipping a physical object.

multicultural: Having many different cultures, or ways of life of different peoples, in a unified society.

nomadic: Having to do with people who move from place to place.

satire: A type of comedy that shows the weaknesses of something.

surreal: Very strange or unusual, like a dream.

urban: Relating to a city.

FOR MORE INFORMATION

BOOKS:

Beckman, Rosina. *The History of Russia from 1801 to the Present.* New York, NY: Britannica Educational Publishing, 2019.

Berge, Anna. *Russia ABCs: A Book About the People and Places of Russia.* Bloomington, MN: Picture Window Books, 2004.

Ganeri, Anita. *Journey Through Russia.* London, UK: Franklin Watts, 2017.

WEBSITES:

Central Asia Facts for Kids
kids.kiddle.co/Central_Asia
This site features information about the history and culture of Central Asia.

Russia Facts for Kids
www.kids-world-travel-guide.com/russia-facts.html
This site provides a basic overview of Russia and its culture.

Russian Culture: Facts, Customs, & Traditions
www.livescience.com/44154-russian-culture.html
This website offers readers a glimpse into Russian cultural traditions.

INDEX

A

Armenia 5, 32
Azerbaijan 5, 16, 32

B

Belarus 5, 16, 17. 24
Bulgakov, Mikhail 27, 30

C

Chekhov, Anton 27

D

Dostoyevsky, Fyodor 26, 27

E

Eisenstein, Sergey 36, 37
Estonia 5

G

Georgia 5

K

Kasparov, Garry 44
Kazakhstan 5, 8, 11, 16, 32, 40
Kournikova, Anna 42
Kyrgyzstan 5, 11, 16, 40

L

Latvia 5
Lithuania 5

M

Moldova 5

N

Nava'i, Ali Shir 25

P

Pavlova, Anna 33
Prokofiev, Sergey 34, 37
Pushkin, Aleksandr 25, 26

S

Solzhenitsyn, Aleksandr 30
Soviet Union (USSR) 4, 5, 11, 13, 15, 21, 22, 24, 30, 36, 37, 41
Stalin, Joseph 5, 21, 22, 31, 36

T

Tajikistan 5, 40
Tarkovsky, Andrey Arsenyevich 37, 38
Tchaikovsky, Pyotr Ilyich 34, 35
Tolstoy, Leo 26, 29
Turkmenistan 5, 16

U

Ukraine 5, 8, 9, 16, 17, 21
Uzbekistan 5, 8, 15, 16